STRAIGHT TO
HAPPY

WESTCOM PRESS

Washington DC

STRAIGHT TO
HAPPY

Discovering the Power of Choice
to Maximize Your Life

Cynthia Mabry

Straight to Happy

© 2013 Cynthia Mabry

www.StraightHappy.com

Printed in United States of America

ISBN: 978-1-9386200-2-7

Library of Congress Control Number: 2012951105

First Edition

Printed in the United States of America
18 17 16 15 14 13 12   1 2 3 4 5

Published by: Westcom Press
           2101 N Street, NW, Suite T-1
           Washington, DC 20037
           westcom.press@mac.com

Table of Contents

Introduction

It was a beautiful evening on the beach. The moon was full, the air warm and inviting. My husband and I had just celebrated our niece's wedding with his entire family—siblings, friends. We had all traveled from Nashville, Tennessee, to Destin, Florida, for this special event. A few of us actually chose to take the week before as vacation, renting a house on the beach, leaving the night of the wedding as our last evening in Destin. Returning to the beach house after the ceremony was the last time I would see my husband alive.

The next time I saw him, he had passed out from doing an unknown number of Jäger bombs with the best man—chasing shots of Jägermeister with Red Bull. His sister and I moved him onto the floor of our bedroom at the beach house and decided to go back out for our last walk on the beach. When we returned, the smell of vomit almost knocked us down it was so potent. My husband and the best man had both regurgitated while passed out—there is no telling how much they drank. When I found my husband, he had stopped breathing, and his arm was turning blue. We immediately called 911.

I curled into a fetal position under the kitchen table and rocked back and forth while the paramedics tried for what seemed like a lifetime to revive my Rob. When they carried him out on the stretcher, I knew he was gone.

I went into shock . . . I was numb. I don't remember much about the next eight weeks with the exception of two events—I had to tell Rob's son that his father was dead, and I had to arrange a funeral for my husband. Everything else is a blur. I completely shut down.

Have you seen the movie *P.S. I Love You*? That was my life. I was twenty-nine when I suddenly lost my husband, and then I lost my job (what I thought was my career). Like in the movie, my family and closest friends threw me a thirtieth birthday party, a surprise party. And, like the main character, Holly, I reinvented myself.

In the last several years, since coming out of my fog, I have been forever changed. Once a shy introvert, timid and insecure, I've transformed into a strong and outgoing woman. After all, I now have nothing else to lose. I no longer recognize the person I used to be, and for that I am grateful. My life today is much more enriched, full of life and love and joy. I've let go of the people and things that were a constant killjoy and now focus on simply being happy, regardless. Unfortunately, most people don't go straight to happy. Most people think of success and happiness as conflicting forces. Why? We've been conditioned to believe that success is a destination, a result. I want to explore looking at success as a journey, with happiness its companion, and challenge you to adopt that belief.

In this book, I will take you through a holistic approach to create balance in all areas of life—this leads to ultimate happiness and inner peace. Throughout the pages that follow, you will read several stories from my personal life and how each has shaped and molded me into the person I am today. Each experience in life forms peaks and valleys, some higher and deeper than others. You see, it takes all different experiences to reach a point of true contentment with where we are on this journey of life. By sharing with you many of my experiences, it is my hope that you will relate to at least one and allow me to provide guidance in your next steps.

I hope you will find as much value as I did in each of the exercises in this book. They are by no means original ideas but a compilation of methods I have discovered throughout my quest to know more about myself. Each chapter is devoted to what I believe are the most vital ways to bring awareness of your current life to the forefront so that you can challenge yourself, stretch yourself, and make a decision to *live* your life instead of just existing. To provide another way of looking at situations, another way of reacting to life events, another choice, another chance to go straight to happy.

Chapter 1

Three Little Words

The myth of happy . . . why is it a myth? Do people really believe that we are meant to suffer? Who are these people? Is happiness a result? Why do we even think this way? One could argue that everything we do and think has been conditioned. And for the most part that is absolutely true.

But why? I mean really—*why*?

I have become a serial questioner of life. I love nothing more in life than to learn and absorb, implement if necessary, and repeat. Have you noticed how the most successful approaches in life are as simple as shampooing? Lather, rinse, repeat. In my journey these last several years, self-education has revealed so much more to me than anything I learned through all my formal education.

I put myself through a community college program and discovered that college just wasn't for me. I believe in formal education when one is going for a specific profession or trade, such as a doctor, lawyer, CPA, nurse, and so on. I don't see the point, however, in going to school for four years, accumulating tens of thousands of dollars in debt, only to graduate with a general business degree.

Traditional education is not a requirement for happiness and success, but that doesn't mean learning and educating yourself aren't necessary. Without an open mind, however, this learning is nearly impossible, and therefore growth, success, and happiness are much more difficult to reach.

I Know That!

Allow me to give you a brief background: I come from a family of medicine. My father runs the heart-lung machine during open heart surgery. The technical name for what he does is perfusionist, but whenever I use that word, the next question is always "what's *that*?" So I begin with the descriptive—saves time. My mom is an MBA, a BS, an RN, and a CNOR, and she has been a surgical nurse and an educator for most if not all of my life. My stepmom is a nurse practitioner. My stepsister is an RN and recently became a flight nurse—how cool is that? My other stepsister is a licensed practical nurse, or LPN. She actually took her certification classes from my mom!

We lived in a small town in Kentucky—does that answer your next question?

Needless to say, my younger sister and I grew up with roundtable discussions of open heart surgery as we chewed our meatloaf and potatoes. Dinner was always interesting when we were kids. So what happened to me and my sister? We ended up as the geeks in the family. Yes, geeks! I dove into telecommunications and marketing, and she knows software like nobody's business. I am guessing we absorbed enough information to be perfusionists by default. I mean, it certainly seemed that way.

When I first attended community college, I thought I would go into another area of medicine, sports medicine. I loved football and basketball, and this would keep medicine in the family. After my first two years, however, I lacked seventeen credit hours because I was working full time to put myself through school. So I picked what classes I could that would allow me to graduate and changed my associate degree from sports medicine to health and wellness—what my parents had always wanted. I was done with the classroom, where I'd been surrounded by the familiar topics I'd grown up learning about from my family. I remember thinking at the time, *I know all that.*

Have you ever heard someone say, "I know that"? Did you know that those are the three most dangerous words in the history of communication? I'm not kidding. Think about it. When you are explaining yourself, or an idea, or you are super excited about a new opportunity or possibility, and the person you are talking to says, "I know that," what does that do to you? Do you want to shout, "No, you don't!" More important, what does it say about that person? When people utter these words, they are completely closed off to anything new. Their minds are blocked, their eyes shut, and their hearts surrounded by a 100-foot wall. They are at a mental and emotional dead end.

Think about the numerous times *you* have uttered these words. I know I used to—all the time. And the phrase said everything about me and where I was on my journey, which wasn't very far, obviously. "I know that" says everything about your attitude, your motivation, and most important, your communication skills.

Straight Talk

Take a moment to reflect on the times you may have uttered "I know that" or something similar.

- What were the circumstances?
- Who were you talking to?
- Do you remember the conversation? What were you talking about?
- What do you remember learning from that conversation?

More than likely you were tense and 100 percent defensive, which results in 100 percent unproductive dialogue.

As you go through the remaining chapters of this book, try to keep your mind open to new ideas and perspectives. You certainly don't have to agree, but it's important to acknowledge them and at least consider the possibility that they might hold truth for you. If you catch yourself thinking or even saying, "I know that," step back for a second. Reread . . . then continue.

Letting Go

Another way we close our minds to learning—and to happiness—is by beating ourselves up. This may seem like the opposite of saying, "I know that," but they both stem from insecurities and fears. After all, it takes more courage and confidence to admit we don't know everything than to pretend—even to ourselves—that we do.

This book discusses some difficult topics, including the need to look at your life unflinchingly so that you can be honest with yourself about what you need to change. But being honest and beating yourself up are not the same thing. Just the opposite, actually. Often, we beat ourselves up so that we don't have to face the truth. We can punish ourselves instead with negative thoughts about everything we've done and haven't done. These thoughts only get in the way of discovering how to use our truths, even the painful truths, to lead us in a new, positive direction.

Many of us formed the habit of beating ourselves up after being hurt—a hurt we haven't learned to let go. But if you never let it go, how will you know where to begin? The smallest shifts in our beliefs and values can amount to extraordinary changes in our own lives and in the lives of those around us.

Let those words go!

Action Steps

The Law of Vacuum goes something like this: The universe cannot put good into your hand until you let go of what you are holding in it. Put another way—release the crap! If you don't, the universe cannot deliver. Ask yourself these questions for each area of your life (health, relationships, finance, business/career, personal/spiritual development, lifestyle/environment, etc.):

- What am I holding onto in this area of my life?
- What am I doing that's not working?

In fact, I encourage you to consider what you're doing that *is* working but that leaves you feeling so-so, as though you settled. Good enough doesn't lead to happiness.

Are you willing to give up good for *great*?

Chapter 2

What Safety Net?

One piece of advice I can give out of the gate that is worth more than ten times the cost of this book is this: If you are married or have children, you must—that is *must*—have life insurance and a will. Why do I say this? My husband and I did not have either. Stupid, you say . . . how naive. Yes, I was naive. I was twenty-four when I married. I was physically unable to bear children, and my husband had a son from a previous marriage. What did I need life insurance for? Certainly nothing would happen to *me*. Boy, was I wrong.

In the days and weeks following the death of my husband, I was blessed beyond belief to be surrounded by family and friends who took care of me, because I was physically and mentally unable to care for myself. I took a three-month break from life, then decided to get back in the game. I couldn't be the spinster—that wasn't me. I have always been a somewhat optimistic person, but I didn't have the tools to create an optimistic mindset out of the depths of despair I felt I had been thrown into.

So I went back to my job, working for a telecommunications company I had been with for seven years strong. When I returned from my leave of absence, many changes were under way. We had been bought—again. Sound familiar? Can you guess what's coming next? You got it. My department was being moved from the operations side of the house to IT, and with that move, my department's positions were being absorbed (i.e., eliminated). I was looking at a severance package not even three weeks after returning to my "career."

All I could remember thinking was "Seriously?!" So not only had I just lost my husband, I had no insurance, no will, no contingency fund (most people call this an emergency fund), and now no career. I couldn't cry. I couldn't be upset. I simply accepted it for what it was. After all, I had no control over my employers' moves and decisions. But I did have control over how I reacted to them. It served no purpose to get mad or angry or throw a fit—all things I would have contemplated doing just seven months prior. All in all, this was truly a blessing. Between the severance pay and my husband's death benefit from his employer, the cost of the funeral and transportation services were covered, and I even managed to pay off a credit card we shared.

A Blessing in Disguise

So what next? I took a break. I started teaching dance again full time, I created a Facebook account, I took my stepson on a cruise (where I met someone who has remained one of my dearest friends to this day), I visited with family, I went to movies, I watched pay-per-view movies, I slept, I listened to music, I started playing music again. I did whatever I wanted. And that's when it hit me: I had just tasted *freedom* for the first time. I had never known what that meant before.

Since I was fifteen years old, I had always had a job. I moved out on my own at eighteen and put myself through college. Other people had always controlled my minutes, hours, and days. Other people had always controlled how much I made, when I had to show up for work, and whether I was *allowed* to take a day off. If I went above and beyond on my daily duties, trading my time for money, I *might* be eligible for a 5 percent raise ... and that's only if I exceeded expectations.

That's a lot of blood, sweat, and tears that went down the drain with my severance package. I had busted my rump all those years for twelve weeks of "thank you" pay. Really?! That's when I knew that the past fifteen years of modern-day slavery I had endured were over.

Having a job isn't a safety net—it's the largest gamble you could ever take.

Working day after day after day, year after year, countless hours of overtime, only I was a salaried employee, so I got the opportunity to work over forty hours a week all the time and not be compensated for it. All to walk into work one day and be told that my department's positions were being absorbed. I bet you can think of a few choice words that ran through my head. All the words you just thought of probably came out of my mouth too. Every emotion you can think of, I felt. But would you believe one of them was relief? That's right. I said relief.

The entire time I had been with that company, at my many desks, on just about every floor and in every building, I spent most of the day communicating with Rob via email or chat messaging. And the brief time I was at work after my return from leave, that's all that went through my head—the time of day, what I would have been chatting with him about, what I would have made us for dinner that we both might have brought in for lunch the next day. I lived in the world of "what if" for all of three weeks, and I was going insane.

So yes, being let go was a blessing.

Losing my job forced me to think about what in the heck I *really* wanted to do. Did I want to program toll-free numbers, run scheduling for call centers, and manage other people the rest of my life? Or did I want to pursue and be a part of something bigger than little ol' me?

Something that got me out of bed every morning excited about my day, every day. What a concept!

The hunt was on.

Just Ask

Now, as you know, rarely does someone pursue their dreams and actually succeed the first go-round. Such was my experience. But I possess something—the desire to leave a legacy, to create a shift in the way people think about "this happened to me" so that they focus instead on "how am I going to react to what happens?" . . . and to not give up until I do. A lot of people know how this higher calling feels, and many have been successful thought leaders, shaping the very way we think today. Since I believe in not reinventing the wheel, I was on a mission to find them, learn from them, and be a sponge.

In the meantime, I had to support myself.

My phone rang the following February. Can you guess who it was? Why, it was my old company asking me to come back on board. Seems their plans to cut resources weren't working out quite as they had hoped. Hello, opportunity knocking. I opened that door and *danced* through it. I didn't accept their offer to be a "part of the team" again—not on their terms anyway—but I needed income to live, and I was overqualified for the jobs I had been applying for. So I negotiated. I agreed to come back as a private contractor and at a 50 percent increase in pay.

That initial six-month contract was extended for over three years. It seems my services were needed.

Straight Talk

What areas of your life can you afford to take risks in? Be bold! Are you in a job where you feel under-valued? Have you been laid off in the last twelve months? Consider contracting privately—this gives you a set amount of time at a price you can nego-tiate, either hourly or per contract. It also gives you a glimpse into the world of establishing yourself as a business owner and the beginning of the greatest incorporation ever known: You, Inc.

Instead of sitting on a log wondering what in the heck I was going to do, or thinking that being a full-time employee was my only option, I chose to look at things differently, and I took a chance by asking if they would be willing to contract. What's the worst they could have said? No? But if I hadn't asked, then the answer would have been no by default. This one shift in how I thought about my situation and how I was going to react to it has forever changed my life. I realized the importance of self-worth. I boosted my own self esteem—the corporate world has certainly never done that! But most important, I learned to ask.

Action Item

Learn to become a serial questioner. Asking is a strength, not a weakness. Ask for help. Ask for what you want. If you never ask, the answer is always no.

What do you want but are afraid to ask for in your personal life and in your professional life? Commit to asking yourself at least one of these questions this week:

- Am I compensated fairly for my work?
- Am I valued in my workplace?
- Does my family express gratitude for the things I do for them?
- Do I feel loved?

Chapter 3

Habitually Unhappy

*H*ave you ever noticed how some people always have something to complain about? Why? I meant what is the point? Some people get out of bed and immediately have a bad attitude. The weather isn't right, or maybe they overslept, or just the day of the week is bothering them. Then they leave the house and complain about traffic and have road rage the entire way to the office. Once at the office, they can't help but complain to their cubicle farm about how lazy the new person is or how they always have to do the work of the entire team . . . life is so unfair. Come lunchtime, there is never anything to eat. And the list goes on and on and on and on. It's wearing me out just writing it. How draining is that? And we're only up to lunch! I think you get my point.

You may have heard this one before: Change your thoughts, change your life. Believe it? You should. It's 100 percent truth.

Habits of Mind

I want to share the story of my friend—I'll call her Amanda. I met Amanda when I was twenty-two. We both worked for the same company. We weren't close the first few years, not for any other reason than we worked in separate departments. From afar, Amanda was the life of the party. She was beautiful, funny, slightly abrasive, and sharp as a tack. Everyone loved her, and life was grand.

When some shifts occurred among departments, we ended up working closely together in management roles. I got to know Amanda on a personal level—we spent time together outside of work, and a group of us went to lunch almost every day. Amanda joked a lot, but I noticed that she was pretty discouraged or irritated in every area of her life. She had an abusive relationship with her mother; her ex-husband was always creating problems, it seemed; then it was her ex-husband's new wife; and the management at work was always out to get her. It seemed there was no pleasing Amanda unless she had a cigarette to puff on and food to not eat. These were not only my observations but those of her best friend, Diane, as well. Diane and I had gotten close by association, and the more we shared, the clearer our theory became—Amanda was habitually unhappy.

Amanda was relentless about how much she struggled daily. Being a single mom, she was the sole provider for several years until she was awarded some support from the youngest girls' dad. Nonetheless, even when his help kicked in, she constantly struggled. She focused on what she didn't have and what was wrong with her life in almost every thought, be it not enough money, unreliable cars, people out to get her at work, her lazy, good-for-nothing ex-husband, his new wife creating drama, and on and on and on it went.

Can you see the theme? Amanda's inner world (thoughts) was literally creating her outer world. It's so easy to see from the outside looking in—isn't that always the case though?

Actions Speak Louder Than Words

The hardest time in my friendship with Amanda was after my husband passed away. I was in a dark place for months, and around the time I started coming out of it, I reached out to her to reconnect. All I could remember was that she made me laugh and that I could always count on her for an honest answer. We reconnected, starting talking at length on the phone again, and so on. Then came the call that changed our relationship forever. She was being evicted from her home, and she was hysterical. What was she going to do with her two daughters? Live out of her car? Living with her warped mother was out of the question. I was living in my four-bedroom house by myself and was yearning for companionship. I opened up my home to her and her girls over the summer. It would be great. A win-win for us all. For the first few months, this was the case. We shared household duties, had pool parties and movie marathons. To boot, Amanda loved to clean, which was absolutely fine with me!

Over the course of her stay with me, however, I started to truly see the inner workings of Amanda's mind. Even though I had opened up my home to help her and her girls, she started complaining about how far out my house was, how long the drive was, that the girls didn't like being out here . . . the complaints rolled in nonstop. I even tried to open Amanda up to my world, sharing my experiences, trials, outcomes, and how I chose to think about them. Things and people only have power over you if you allow them to.

She detested this about me. Truly resented it. So I finally quit talking to her altogether about her problems. If she started venting about how all was wrong in her world, I would go in my bedroom and close the door. I eventually quit coming home until I knew they were all in bed just so I didn't have to listen to the crap.

I decided to take a break from it all and went on a cruise with a dear friend. When I got off the boat, I turned my cell phone on to a frantic message from Amanda. Her dog had died, and she didn't know if she and the girls could stand to be all the way out in the middle of nowhere, in my house where it had happened, for another day—it was drama of epic proportion. I was sad their dog had died. After all, she had become a part of my family as well over the summer. I calmed Amanda down, and we agreed to chat about everything when I got home and we could process it logically.

When I turned into my driveway, the house was completely dark, and her car wasn't there. No big deal. This would give me a chance to unpack and get settled back in. As I walked into the house, the smell of bleach hit me like a ton of bricks. I flipped on the lights to find my home in perfect condition, with no trace of Amanda or her girls. It was as if they had never been there.

And that is when I lost it.

The last time I had felt that wall of emptiness walking into my house was the day I had returned from Florida after Rob passed away. Now, encountering that feeling all over again, I couldn't breathe. I literally had a panic attack. I managed to dial my best friend, and she stayed on the phone with me until she arrived at my house. That's when I clearly saw Amanda's behavior pattern. When things get rough, she bolts. Poor pitiful her. Bad things always happen to her. She would find someone else to believe her story and take care of her. The pattern was as cut and dry as shampooing hair: Lather, rinse repeat.

I felt like a fool for believing her. I was furious. Most of all, I was disappointed in who she *really* was. You see, people will always show you who they are if you let them. Take off your blinders and cover your ears. Start watching what people do and not putting as much stock in what they say.

Victims and Enablers

Remember, we have absolutely no control over many things that happen to us in life, be they burglaries, tornadoes, parents divorcing, people dying, loss of limb functionality . . . I could go on and on. We have no control. The only thing we control is how we react to what happens. Win that battle, and you'll take ownership of your mind—and eventually your life.

I was the enabler in this story. When I opened my heart and home to Amanda, I set in motion her cycle of destruction. How could I have known? I couldn't have. Here's a concept that took me a while to accept: You teach people how to treat you. Whether it's conscious or not, the way others treat you is a reflection of how you believe you should be treated.

> ### *Straight Talk*
>
> Do you walk through life blaming others? In what areas of your life are you giving away your power? To certain people? To situations? Things that have happened to you in the past, maybe?
>
> On the flip side, who are you enabling to act like this in your life?
>
> How are you teaching people to treat you?

Which person do you relate to in this story, the victim or the enabler? Answer that honestly. More than likely you will see it pop up in every avenue of your life: socially, emotionally, physically, and professionally.

As soon as you recognize the role you're playing, you no longer play that role. Let me say that again. As soon as you recognize it, *you are no longer it.* Talk about powerful. Admitting it is the hardest part. After all, if you're not honest with yourself, how can you expect anyone else to be?

Amanda lived in a world that was against her. She had an emotionally unstable childhood and chose to continually be around her mom then complain afterward every time. She could have set boundaries as an adult, for herself, of what she would and would not allow her mom to be a part of, and what she would and would not tolerate. She had choices in how to react, and unfortunately she chose to see herself as a powerless victim.

Amanda always had problems with her ex-husband and, when he remarried, his wife. What was interesting is that through all the problems she claimed were their fault, she was the one with the restraining order against her. Once she was in my home, it was clear who was creating the drama.

Don't create unnecessary crap for your life or the lives of those you care about. Do expect more. If Amanda had really focused on and been grateful for everything she had—from her home to her clothing to her vehicles to her employment—I guarantee she would have attracted more and more good things into her life.

Choose Your Thoughts, Choose Your Life

You have the right to decide what you like and what you don't. You have the choice to focus on the positive instead of the negative. When you expect bad things to happen, the universe will conspire to give you what you're focusing on. Shift your thinking. Focus on the positives. You just might start experiencing more peace.

Action Step

Choosing positive thoughts is a habit that you have to form. The media alone inundates us with horrible, depressing stories, which contribute to our thoughts more than we realize. Take control of your mind. Choosing positive thoughts instead of negative will lead to more positive actions, which is directly proportional to the positive results in your world.

Start noticing the influences on your thinking. Do you watch a lot of news? What do you read for leisure? Do you watch live TV with commercials? Are you around negative people? Did you grow up learning to look at the world in negative ways?

If positive thinking is foreign to you, it might help to make a deliberate effort to write down as many positive thoughts about your present and your future as you can. Look at this list every day and keep adding to it. By practicing positive thinking, you can make it a habit.

Chapter 4

Wake Up!

I want to talk about those who go through the motions. Has anyone ever asked you, "What do you want?" and your reply was "I just want to be happy"? What does that mean? Why aren't you already? What will it take for you to be happy?

At a young age, I was never good with the status quo. While all my friends were knocking off, playing, having sleepovers, I was practicing who I wanted to be. From five to twelve years old, I studied dance. How was I different from any other little girl taking dance class? I didn't just study dance, I *was* dance.

At this point in my life, my family was living in Spartanburg South Carolina—a nice-sized community with many great areas to explore and experience. My mother had enrolled me in classes at an establishment called Miss

Marion's School of Dance. I can still remember the lobby, the changing rooms, and the three dance studios.

Miss Marion had a daughter, Lori. Lori studied ballet at the University of Miami and went on to New York City to become a Rockette before retiring to move back home and start her family. Miss Marion and Lori introduced me to tap dancing, and my world was forever changed. Give me a pair of tap shoes and a concrete floor, and I was set! Make it a wooden floor at the dance studio, and I was in heaven. I loved dance so much that I practiced morning, noon, and night. I even gave up my Saturdays to be in the Carolina Dance Youth Theater. I ended up being asked to join the competition team, competing on a national level, and won—several times. At a very young age, I was already willing to give up good for great.

This theme continued into my early teens. When my parents relocated our family to Madisonville, Kentucky, I was lost without the regimen of tap woven throughout my days. I tried the local dance schools, but I was too advanced. My parents hired a private dance instructor to drive from Indiana, meeting us halfway in Hendersonville. She was a good teacher, but she wasn't versed in Broadway, the style that was a part of my soul. So I made the painful decision to hang up my tap shoes, and I dove into music.

Music had also always been a passion in my life. Both of my parents are musically inclined, and so are my sister and I. I had taken piano from the age of four, and I had practiced for thirty minutes a day, every day of my life. Now, I'm not a modern-day Mozart by any means. This is simply to illustrate the principles instilled in me at a very young age.

The flute had always interested me as well. When we lived in California, watching my mom's friend play the flute in church completely mesmerized me. That was the instrument I wanted to learn to play, and I picked it up in seventh grade. I was a quick study, advancing to first chair and even making the all-state band.

These themes have been a continuous force in my life: I decide what I want, and I do what it takes to obtain it. Never have I thought, "I'm not good enough" or "I'm not smart enough." Anything I have ever wanted to do or experience has *always* been possible. People who claim the victim or are just lazy puzzle me. Seriously, I've never understood it. And if you're reading this book, chances are you feel the same way. We're all looking for something—striving for something—figuring out how to make this world a better place. How to make ourselves better.

Facing the Truth

I'm going to take a turn here, because when I was thirteen, my world was flipped upside down. I can remember the day I walked into my house and my mom and dad told my sister and me that they were divorcing. I went numb. Completely numb. Our family was being broken up, and I was devastated.

The next several years, I continued to excel in my academic work and immersed myself in band—concert and marching. Half the year I was either first, second, or third chair in concert band, and the other half of the year I was marching in the color guard or rifle line. From ages thirteen to sixteen, my life was a blur. I kept myself as busy as I possibly could so that I wouldn't have to feel. That's how I coped—by not feeling.

When staying busy, keeping away from home, and playing music no longer worked as effectively as they once had, I started using narcotics to numb my emotions. I drank, smoked, and started snorting pills that had been prescribed to me for depression. During all of this, I was maintaining the appearance of the good girl—excelling in school, a top performer, and even trying out for the varsity cheerleading squad at the end of my sophomore year—and making the cut.

That next summer I spiraled down and out of control. I was treading water until I came home one morning to find my best friends in the living room with my mom. That's right—I had walked into an intervention.

How had I lost control? What the hell had happened to me? I was admitted into rehabilitation in Evansville, Indiana, where I was moved to two other treatment facilities, out of the "under eighteen" category and into an adult program. They told me drugs weren't my problem. I wanted to scream, "You think, genius?!" Of course, I let my smartass appear from time to time, but for the most part, I encountered brilliant and compassionate people who just wanted to help me.

My addiction was an issue short term, but that was just the overlay. My calculated and superior practice of avoidance was my biggest problem. I had been running for three years: running from my storybook childhood, running from my anger towards my parents for ripping our family apart, running from my sister's pain-stricken face—I was out of steam. I couldn't keep up the facade any longer. And once I faced all this head on, acknowledged it, and worked through it, the hardest part of the battle was won.

Once you face your problems, fears, insecurities— whatever you want to call them—they no longer exist. You may have heard that admitting the problem is the hardest part. It's true, and this is why: It takes a high level of maturity to stand out of your own way and call yourself on your own crap. Not a lot of people can do that.

I learned some of life's toughest lessons while very young—for that I feel extremely fortunate. Did I miss out on some of the best times of my life? Not a chance. Those are still ahead of me.

Straight Talk

Take a few quiet minutes and prepare to be brutally honest with yourself when answering the following questions:

- What areas in your life have challenged you?
- What makes you feel alive?
- What are you afraid of?
- What are you running from?
- If you had six months to live, what would you do?
- What or who inspires you?
- What would you do if you knew you couldn't fail?

Be honest. If there is one area that I challenge people in every day, it is the ability to be completely honest with themselves. Think about it—if you aren't honest with yourself, how in the world can you expect anyone else to be honest with you? It doesn't happen. Learn to be honest with the person staring back at you in the mirror. Only then will you start to reach any level of peace. Control the space between your ears and you control your life.

What Defines You?

Addictions come in all shapes and sizes—narcotics, spending money, gambling, men, women, sex, exercise, food, lack of food, appearance, gossip, TV, Internet, gaming, movies, and last but not least, *drama*. Nearly everyone is addicted to something. It's human nature. One can even be addicted to learning, or the experience of learning. I call them seminar junkies—you know, the people who attend all the seminars but never implement any of the practices in their daily lives.

Self-awareness is undervalued in our culture. If more people were aware of their own habits, society as a whole would be unstoppable. Your daily habits *define* who you are. Think I'm being a bit absolute? Here's another challenge for you.

Action Steps

This exercise is going to be extremely difficult, and you may even have to do it seven, eight, nine, even ten times to get the most accurate results because your conditioned mind will kick in and make you "forget." Ready? What could be so huge an undertaking?

Track an entire day.

That's right. For one whole day, I want you to write down every single activity from the time you wake up to the time you go to sleep. This includes what you eat for breakfast, the time you start working, what are you doing while you work: Are you on the Internet? Are you returning email? Are you mixing in personal email? Are you logged in to Facebook or Twitter? How about Linked-In? Did you eat lunch? How long were you on the computer? When did you leave work? What TV shows did you watch when you got home from work? What did you eat for dinner?

I think you get the point.

This is not an easy task by any stretch of the imagination. But until you have done this, I ask that you not read any further. Because the things we discuss later in the book are contingent on your having completed this exercise.

Have you been wondering why you can't get projects accomplished? Why you aren't meeting the same goals you set for yourself year after year? Why your family has stopped counting on you? Why your friends no longer believe you'll do what you say you're going to do?

Don't beat yourself up! This is the cycle that most people go through, that I went through until I completed tracking an entire day. And what I learned from that exercise *changed my life*. Now stop reading and get ready to change yours.

Chapter 5

Mirror, Mirror on the Wall . . .

*H*ow was the day? Did you find it relatively easy? Hard? I was so frustrated when I did this exercise. I mean, really! Here comes the most adventuresome part of the book—we get to add up all the time that you just documented from your *current* "day in the life." You certainly don't need to count down to the minute—that level of detail is not necessary. I can hear some of you now: "But wait! If I don't get the exact minutes, won't my calculations be skewed or incorrect?" Rest easy. The point is simply to give you a glimpse into your life as it *is*, not how you *think* it is.

If we live to be eighty years old, we get roughly 700,800 hours to live. That's 365 days, times eighty years, times twenty-four hours. This is the time we have to enjoy, to love, to weep, to learn, and to cry. The quest for "the good life," for meaning, for fulfillment, for purpose must fit into these hours. But we spend a lot of our time doing other things, things we think we have little choice in, so we don't pay much attention to them . . . until now.

It All Adds Up

It fascinates me that the vast majority of people are so caught up in what they think their life looks like that they don't see how it actually is. I used to be one of them. Well, I'm getting ready to burst a lot of bubbles. I call them truth bubbles.

Here's a little table to illustrate how much time you'll devote to certain activities over the course of one, five, and fifty years based on how much time you devote to them in an average day.

Per Day	Per Year	Per 5 Years	Per 50 Years
10 minutes	2.5 days	12.5 days	125 days
15 minutes	3.8 days	19 days	190 days
30 minutes	7.6 days	38 days	380 days
1 hour	15.2 days	76 days	760 days
2 hours	30.4 days	152 days	1,520 days

For example, if you average ten minutes per day processing email, you'll spend the equivalent of two and a half twenty-four-hour days processing email this year.

If we looked at this in a work week perspective, two and a half twenty-four-hour days adds up to sixty hours. This means that you're investing more than one and a half full working weeks each year just to processing email. And over the course of fifty years, you'll spend seventy-five weeks, or 1.4 working years, doing nothing but processing email—this is assuming fifty-two weeks per year at forty hours per week, with no vacation time built in!

How easy is it to spend ten minutes or more per day on little ol' email? How about watching TV? Sleeping?

Now, it's your turn. Take a look at all the time you tracked yesterday. Go ahead—tally away. I want you to add up all time spent and list it here in the following areas:

How You Spent Your Day

Sleeping: _____

Watching TV: _____

On the Internet:

    Checking email: _____

    On social media: _____

    Blogging: _____

Commuting to/from work: _____

Working: _____

Reading: _____

Exercising: _____

Preparing meals: _____

Eating: _____

Talking with spouse/significant other: _____

_____

Talking with children: _____

Meditating: _____

Other: _____

So how does your day look? Shocking, isn't it? Are you upset? Bothered? Irritated? Mad as hell? Good! You *should be*. Look at all the time you have been wasting, all the time you could have been spending with your kids, your significant other, reading, learning about a new subject, discovering a new language, playing an instrument, just breathing, and my personal favorite—all the time you could have been working on that project that was going to get you out of the nine-to-five.

Compounding the Problem—and the Solution

Next, we're going to compound all of these areas. Yes— the *C* word. Are you familiar with the "doubling penny" scenario? Let's say someone gave you the following choice:

You can either take $1,000,000 right now, cold hard cash, or take a penny today and let it double every day for thirty days, taking the total on day thirty-one.

So which one would you want?

If you took the $1,000,000, you just sold yourself short. Why? Simply put, the power of compounding. That penny deal would have given you $5.4 million at the end of thirty days. And if you could hold out just one more day, $10.8 million.

Don't believe me? Go to Google and type in "compounding penny"—or better yet, open an excel spreadsheet and calculate thirty days. Or—this is a farfetched idea—get out a piece of paper and a calculator and figure it out. If you are really ambitious, you could use your multiplication skills—but you might have to dust them off first.

So here's how compounding applies to our time-tracking exercise. Assuming most of you are over eighteen, we'll take eighteen years from your current age to compound the total time you have wasted. Ready? If you weren't disturbed before, you're about to be.

First, subtract eighteen from your age, then multiply that number times the amount of time you spend per day on one activity. I'll use myself as an example and the average time people spend watching TV per day, which is four hours.

EXAMPLE

I am 33. Subtract 18 and I have 15 years.

To obtain my total time as an adult wasted to date on watching TV, I take 365 days × 4 hours of TV a day × 15 years.

That's 21,900 hours. There are 8,760 hours in a year. I would have spent 2.5 *years* of the last 15 *watching television*!

Go ahead. Scream. Aaaaaaaah!

Now, repeat this for all areas that you calculated (the tallying, not necessarily the screaming!).

The first step in changing your life is awareness, taking how you think things are and learning how they actually are, comparing what you *think* you do daily to what you *actually* do daily.

Straight Talk

Don't spend a tremendous amount of energy worrying about the time that's already gone. But that doesn't mean ignore it. As if these numbers could be ignored!

Hold on to all these wonderful calculations you just did and *use them* productively as a tool to gauge the areas of your life that you can adjust or eliminate. I personally cut off my TV watching after I did this exercise in November 2010, and I haven't missed it, not one second.

Is it safe to say you are now aware of the time you spend on pointless and meaningless activities? Great. Pat yourself on the back. Let's keep going. (As if we need to take this any further, but you should know by now that I have to continue.)

Tracking Your Fuel

So let me ask some tougher questions: Are you overweight? Tired? Do you suffer from mood swings? I know I sound like an infomercial, but I am completely serious. This is the second part of tracking your day—tracking what you put into your body as fuel. Was anything once fresh? Did you cook anything? Was everything in a package, like a breakfast sandwich or cereal or a bagel? How about bread, lunch meat, and sliced cheese? Potato chips? At dinner, did you actually prepare food? Did you go through drive-thrus all day?

These are all important questions. What you eat is integral to how you feel, the level of energy you have to tackle your day, the ability to think clearly. We need to eat to live, not live to eat. By tracking what we're putting into our bodies, we can then attach physical and emotional reactions to food. Think that is farfetched?

Do you suffer from disease? I used to, but not anymore. I've cured myself of fibromyalgia and hypoglycemia by eliminating the crap I used to call food and actually eating the real stuff—you know, fresh grilled meats, vegetables, fruits, nuts, and cheeses. Get rid of the food that contains all the fillers like high fructose corn syrup and wheat. Here's a challenge for you: Go to your cupboard and try to find a cereal or soup that does not contain wheat. I'd love to hear what you really find.

It all comes down to this: Small changes implemented over and over produce the largest results.

Action Steps

- What activities of your day take up the most amount of time?
- What areas of your life could you trim down or eliminate to make room for other, more fulfilling things or people?

List three changes you are willing to make in the following areas:

- Education/Work

1. _____

   _____

2. _____

   _____

3. _____

   _____

Action Steps (continued)

- Nutrition

1. _____

   _____

2. _____

   _____

3. _____

   _____

- Physical Activity

1. _____

   _____

2. _____

   _____

3. _____

   _____

Now weigh each of these items carefully and decide on the *most important* item from each category. Any more than three changes at a time can be overwhelming, which leads to counter-productivity, and I don't want that for you. I want you to be successful in changing the areas of your life that you *want* to change.

Get three things done, then come back to your list and choose the next one.

The most important part of the Action Steps in this chapter is to verbalize what you are doing. Tell someone the changes you are making and when you are starting. This will hold you accountable because someone else will be able to check in with you to see if you are really following through. This will also force you to be more aware of the choices you are making.

Don't be discouraged if you slip up. The conditioned mind is a hard one to crack, but it *is* possible to do so. Anything is possible when you want it badly enough. Just don't be in the same place you are now one year from today. At least make that promise to yourself. That's progress in the right direction.

Chapter 6

The Average Factor

Have you ever wondered why people run in certain groups? Why the same personality types flock together? Most people don't even pay attention to this. The simple fact is that you are the average of the five people you are around the most. Think it's not true? As human beings, we don't want to admit that outside influences have any control over who we are, the size of our waist, the size of our bank accounts, and how successful we are. You're your own person, right? Well, in a way. You're your own person comprising the people you spend the most time with.

When I started my business back in 2009, I was not hanging out with the kind of people who go for what they want, people who have dreams, who want to challenge the status quo. I was hanging around with people who had been sold the same crap lie that I had—that we had to be employed, mortgage everything from houses to cars, use credit cards at free will, and sock money away in hopes that we might be able to enjoy it by the age of seventy! Sound familiar? Needless to say, when I started my business, I met a ton of resistance: "This will never work!" "Don't you know this is a Ponzi scheme?" "Why aren't you focused on getting a real job?" The list goes on and on and on.

As I started educating myself in business and entrepreneurship, I was hearing more and more that you are who you associate with. So I started looking into it, meaning I had to evaluate my life ... again! Turns out it was spot on. My salary was about $55K a year, I was twenty-five pounds overweight, and I spent most of my day in front of the TV or other media, eating crap food. These were also the characteristics of my best friends and closest family members. What was I supposed to do, just stop talking to them?

I was so nervous about this discovery. How could I tell them I didn't want to be like them? That their negativity and closed minds were no longer welcome? I was so busy looking for validation from my family and friends that I had lost all focus on what I personally held in high regard, such as my integrity and ability to decide what is best for me. I had some very hard conversations with quite a few people and conveyed to them that I was no longer living my life looking for their acceptance.

Once I made it about me and not about them, it became clear that this wasn't "bad" or "good." It was what it was. The desire to be accepted is human. What I had to learn was that I am in complete control of what I allow to go into my head and body. It is all my choice. All of it—from my thoughts to the news to the Internet to the food I put in my mouth—all the way to the complete acceptance I had to come to that my life is what it is, and I am the one who has to live with it.

Trust Yourself

It makes me crazy now to think that I was once one of the flock, one of the sheep, going along with everything I was told as if it were law and could not be challenged. I started diving into my own education, focusing on what I knew would be my way out. I had tunnel vision. Nothing anyone said could deter me any longer from what I wanted and what I started to make happen.

It's perfectly acceptable to stand in your power and let someone know when you aren't okay with something going on. Learn to listen to yourself. Turn your attention inward. *Trust* yourself.

Straight Talk

Sometimes the people closest to you will hold you back the most . . . if you let them. What are you allowing to happen to you? Are you a person of circumstance? A victim of poor choices earlier in life? Are you settling?

As we get older, most of us lose the belief that we can do anything we want. Think about kids in kindergarten: They all have the highest aspirations—to be an astronaut, a doctor, a nurse, an architect, a firefighter, a rock star, a gymnast. And they truly believe that they can be these things with every ounce of their being.

The problem is, somewhere between middle school and high school, most kids are repeatedly told all the things they *can't* do, and the focus is turned there instead of on all the things that are possible. Let's look into your surroundings to see where your energy and attention are focused—or not focused.

The following exercise, What's Your Average, serves several purposes, the first obviously being awareness of who you spend the most time around. Second, the exercise can help you look at why you have these relationships. Are they lifelong friends? Associated by marriage? Ask yourself this question about each one: Does this person add value to my life?

If the answer is yes, they get to stay. If the answer is no, you must start distancing yourself in order to grow.

The people you spend the most time with should be lifting you higher, encouraging you to chase your dreams, being honest with you when you ask for feedback, not just telling you what you want to hear. These people should also be living the life *you want*. I cannot stress that enough.

The Average Factor

What's Your Average?

Take note of the people you are with the most every day. This will include co-workers, family, friends— think of ten names or so. Now I want you to go through the list, identify the top five, and jot them down here:

1. _____

2. _____

3. _____

4. _____

5. _____

Next, I want you to evaluate the following about each person:

- Are they active or sedentary?
- Do they take care of their bodies?
- What kinds of food do they consume?
- Are they a proponent of learning?
- Are they open minded?
- Are they spiritual?
- What is their salary?
- Do they have a lot of debt?
- What do their relationships look like? Are they strong? Abusive?

Take the answers to every question from each person and combine them. You should be looking at a description of yourself. When it comes to salary, add the numbers up and divide by five to get the average. How close is this to your salary? Scary, isn't it?

Should you completely cut ties with people who don't serve you? Some think yes, but I don't believe that is necessary. Personally, I think loving them from a distance is best, because I want to inspire people to live more, do more, be more, and if I can live my life in such a manner for that to happen, then I have done what I'm here to do.

You really *can* have it all. You just have to decide what "it" is, and then decide to not stop until you have it.

Action Steps

What do you want in life? What kind of income would enable you to be financially free of the rat race? What kind of home do you want to surround yourself with? What kind of health are you looking for? What kind of romantic relationship do you want?

How are these things modeled in your environment, in the people you spend time with, in the way you spend your day? In what specific ways can you surround yourself more with what inspires you to create the life you want?

Chapter 7

Be Open. Decide. Be Free.

What is it you want . . . really? Have you stopped to even ask yourself what it is that you want? Do you even know where to begin? This is the problem for most people. Not only has the majority not asked themselves what they want, they throw up their hands in defeat before they ever get started. Sound familiar?

I, too, used to be one of the majority. I went to work, came home, made dinner, tended to laundry, only to wake up the next morning and do it all over again. The only variable to permanently change my perspective was the death of my husband. Sad, isn't it? I can't imagine where I would be today had that not occurred. Some of you reading this are probably thinking, "I can't believe she just said that!" It took me a long time not to feel guilty when uttering that statement. It does not mean anything other than what it is. These are the facts: I was a robot living an automatic life of constant repeat. If my husband were alive today, we might still be in the same cycle, or maybe not at all. Another thing I've stopped doing is the "what if" scenarios; they serve zero purpose. It's not bad or good—it is what it is!

I can't ever imagine living my life that way again. I now see how deprived I was—caught up in the "what ifs" and "whens"—hindsight is always perfect vision, yes? And I am passionate about this: No one should have to wait for a life-altering experience to better themselves or their situation. You will change your life out of desperation or our out of inspiration—I hope to be the inspiration.

Ultimate Blueprint for Life

So how do you move into action? Below is a simple strategy to implement anytime, anywhere. I call this the Ultimate Blueprint for Life. It consists of four basic questions to get you on the path to your ultimate life.

1. What do you *really* want?
2. How do you plan to achieve it?
3. What obstacles could appear and how will you overcome these obstacles?
4. What are the first steps?

Let's walk through each question individually.

What do you really want?

A simple way to determine what you want is to decide. Stop. Go back and read that again. What, were you looking for a big secret? Sorry, there isn't one. If there's one thing that baffles me, it is when people complain over and over and over about how their situation isn't improving, yet they won't change anything they are doing to alter the outcome. Wait—that's the definition of insanity!

Make a decision to be better, to leave this world a better place than when you entered it. If you touch one person's life, you've done your job. Do me one favor—better yet, do this for yourself: Stop talking about what you're going to do and start doing it. I rarely listen to what people say. I find it much more fascinating to watch what they do. Try it for a week. Listen to your family, neighbors, co-workers—and take a closer look at their actions. Speaks volumes, yes?

Now turn your eyes from other people to yourself. It's time to decide for *you*. What areas in your life are non-negotiable? Your health? Your finances? Your relationships? Your happiness? Your spirituality? Make a list of all areas in your life and define in each area one thing that you *want*. Then decide to make it non-negotiable. It really is that simple.

Non-negotiable Goals

For each area of life, write down what you want most, what is non-negotiable for you.

Health: _____

_____

Relationships: _____

_____

Finance: _____

_____

Business/Career: _____

_____

Personal & Spiritual Development: _____

_____

Lifestyle/Environment: _____

_____

Let's take one of my own "wants" as an example for you. Health and nutrition have been of interest to me for as long as I can remember. My entire life I was active—dancing, playing softball, jogging, biking, hiking—but I always battled weight and health issues. My weight would balloon up and down. I have had severe issues with my reproductive system, resulting in a complete hysterectomy at the age of twenty-seven—after that my weight skyrocketed to 160 pounds, putting me at borderline obese, standing at five feet, five inches, and wearing a women's size 16. This was all in addition to the fibromyalgia I battled, starting in my early twenties.

After living in pain for a decade, I started researching how food affects the body, and everything pointed to gluten. Now I had talked about going gluten-free for close to a year, but that's all it was—lip service. I didn't know where to begin or how to incorporate the change. I decided to make being healthy and off pain medication non-negotiable. But I needed a specific, manageable plan.

What is your plan?

My plan to reach these goals comprised three specific tasks: to be gluten-free, to continue walking two miles a day, and to incorporate strength training three times a week.

I realize this is extreme for most, so think about where you are and where you want to be. What is something you

59

can incorporate to reach your non-negotiable goal? Are
you overweight and currently living a sedentary lifestyle?
Would you like to become more active? If so, what is your
plan to get there? Would walking twenty minutes a day
five days a week help? Of course.

Your Life Plan

Write down your plan for achieving your non-negotiable goal in each area of your life. Remember to be
specific.

Health:

- _____

- _____

- _____

Relationships:

- _____

- _____

- _____

Finance:

- _____

- _____

- _____

Your Life Plan (continued*)*

Business/Career:

- _____

- _____

- _____

Personal & Spiritual Development:

- _____

- _____

- _____

Lifestyle/Environment:

- _____

- _____

- _____

What obstacles could appear and how will you overcome them?

After defining what you want and your plan to achieve it, the next step is to anticipate the obstacles you may face. All sorts of variables can pop up, including situations and people, that make it easy to deviate from the things we truly want. That is why they are called obstacles!

It's important to ask yourself, "What could possibly happen to interfere with my plan?" This is an odd step for most, including me. During the years of growth after losing my husband, I had to keep myself from playing the "what if" game, and now I was doing exactly that, but proactively? How weird! Think about it like this—these are all steps to design your *life*. By identifying obstacles and how to overcome them, you are building confidence and defining strategies to respond rather than impulsively react.

Here is an example of an obstacle and a way to overcome it, using my plan for my health.

> **Obstacle:** I could be in an accident, resulting in the loss of my mobility.
>
> **Overcoming:** Stay the course with being gluten-free and move whatever I can, even if it's just a finger or toe wiggle.

Seem silly? Kind of! Then again, so does the idea of creating a life plan . . . just go with it.

Straight Talk

Not convinced that you need to think about problems before you even get started? Here's another perspective:

Let's say the architect of a building did not take into account how the structure would fall in the event of an earthquake. Knowing this, would you want to be in that building? The probability sure goes down, doesn't it?

The same applies to your life. If you don't take the time to consider what could happen as you strive for your goals and what you could do to respond that would enable you to continue toward your desired result, what is the probability that you will stay on course? The probability goes down.

Keep in mind that this is not about focusing on the negative. It's about developing solutions now so that you can bypass the negative during the most difficult part—actually working toward your goals.

Overcoming Obstacles

Take a little time to define what could go wrong with the plan you outlined for each area of your life.

Health

Obstacle: _____

Overcoming: _____

Obstacle: _____

Overcoming: _____

Relationships

Obstacle: _____

Overcoming: _____

Obstacle: _____

Overcoming: _____

Finance

Obstacle: _____

Overcoming: _____

Obstacle: _____

Overcoming: _____

Overcoming Obstacles (continued)

Business/Career

Obstacle: _____

Overcoming: _____

Obstacle: _____

Overcoming: _____

Personal & Spiritual Development

Obstacle: _____

Overcoming: _____

Obstacle: _____

Overcoming: _____

Lifestyle/Environment

Obstacle: _____

Overcoming: _____

Obstacle: _____

Overcoming: _____

What are the first steps?

Taking the first steps to implement a plan can be intimidating—sometimes downright scary! But when you don't think through the initial steps to take, the idea of your great plan and what you want can quickly overwhelm you. You might be thinking, "How will I ever get there?" or "This is too much!"

Breathe.

Breathe again.

Feel better? Whenever you start panicking, just stop and take an open-mouth breath. This recenters your body, brings your heart rate back to normal, and allows you to think a little more clearly.

Now, back to first steps. Let's say we're going to bake a cheesecake. What would the first step be? The list of ingredients? No, that's a few steps ahead of the first one. How about deciding what kind of cheesecake and then obtaining the recipe? Yes.

In my health example, my first steps were a little different because I had already done the research on gluten and knew the foods I could eat in abundance. I had also already been walking two miles a day, but I wanted to continue and add in strength training. My first steps were to learn what foods contained gluten and then clean the gluten out of my house. I then created a tracking sheet so that I could hold myself accountable to my new lifestyle.

And you know what? It worked.

I have been gluten-free since August 15, 2011, and I exercise six days a week. As a result, I am off all pain medications, have not had one migraine, and am sleeping better than I have in twenty years, with more energy to boot. I have successfully achieved what I said I wanted. Small changes, implemented every day, over time produce incredible results. Who knew it could be so easy?

It can be this easy for you as well. Simply decide and take the first step.

We all have goals and dreams, but most of us have not been taught how to bring them to fruition. Everyone designs and plans vacations—why wouldn't you put the same amount of energy into designing your life? The simple layout of the Ultimate Blueprint for Life is something you can use for the rest of your entire life. Revisit it at least once a year. When you achieve something that you planned, fantastic! Reward yourself and keep moving forward by taking another look at what you want *next*.

You see, we never stop improving . . . we never stop growing. We are not perfect. There is always something to strive for. Think of your journey in life like a plant. If a plant isn't growing, it's dying. We are no different. The moment you cease to learn and grow, you begin to die. Be more. Do more. Have more.

First Steps

What are the very first steps to take in your plan to achieve each non-negotiable goal? Write them down below.

Health:

1. _____

2. _____

3. _____

Relationships:

1. _____

2. _____

3. _____

Finance:

1. _____

2. _____

3. _____

First Steps (continued)

Business/Career:

1. _____

2. _____

3. _____

Personal & Spiritual Development:

1. _____

2. _____

3. _____

Lifestyle/Environment:

1. _____

2. _____

3. _____

Action Steps

Would you believe you can design your ultimate life in just one week? It's completely doable. Take just one hour out of each day for one week to complete your life plan. There are six areas of life to go through: Health, Relationships, Financial, Business/Career, Personal and Spiritual Development, and Lifestyle/Environment. Focus on one each day and review on the seventh.

Take the first step in designing your life. Step into the role of conscious creator and *choose* what *you* want your life to look like. Don't accept the norm that most of society conforms to. Life is what you make it—make your life plan non-negotiable starting now.

In Closing

I hope that sharing things I've learned has helped you learn a little something about yourself, and that you will decide to stop making happiness contingent on anything or anyone else and just go straight to happy.

In my quest for knowledge in the past year, I had the opportunity to meet one of the most wonderful women I've ever met, someone I will be connected to for the length of my existence: Annetta Wilson. Annetta and I were attending a workshop in L.A. and ended up sharing a room during our time there. She is simply amazing. I have so much respect for her both personally and professionally. She is one of those people living where I want to be.

One of the many things I learned by knowing Annetta is that no matter where we are on this journey, no matter what success we have, there is *always* room for improvement, always a chance to be better today than yesterday. Always.

During that weekend, Annetta shared an original piece, and it moved me so much that I asked her if I could share it in my book, and she graciously agreed. I hope you will enjoy it as much as I do.

Changing Course

How many times have you made a promise to yourself only to wish later that you'd never set that intention?

What if it was okay that you didn't keep your promise? What if the fact that you didn't keep it was perfect? What if the things that happened, in spite of the promise, were exactly what should have happened?

The proof: *These events showed up, and you're still here!* Give yourself credit for that.

We often get caught up in our "story" about the things that don't go as planned. We tell ourselves that we "should" have done this or that we "ought" to have known better. Rarely do we stop long enough to give ourselves credit for switching course, changing direction, or rolling with the punches.

We hear the stories about tough times and doom and gloom. And while it's true that we may have to make some changes we didn't anticipate, those changes don't have to define who we are. Easier said than done? Yes. But it can be done.

Start making a list of what went *right* over the past twelve months. Who came into your life and made it better? Who walked away and made it better? What did you learn about yourself that wouldn't have been possible except for the circumstances that showed up? Who or what surprised you in an amazing way?

What do you absolutely know to be true?

What do I know? I know that fear and worry can be paralyzing or mobilizing. It depends on where your head is at the time. I know that people are doing the best they can, even when they're not. I know that the only moment change can happen is now. Not yesterday or tomorrow. *Now.*

I know that I've learned more than I thought possible over the past twelve months, met new people who have become treasured friends, and lost people I will miss forever. I've come to understand that just because something shows up that I don't like doesn't mean I can't appreciate the lesson, eventually.

More than anything, I've learned to give myself credit for not giving up or giving in. Sometimes, that's the difference between twelve months of regret and twelve months of gratitude.

What kind of year will you choose?

About Annetta Wilson

Annetta Wilson is a business strategist specializing in communication skills, presentation skills, and media training. She has coached on-air journalists at CNN and coached for Walt Disney World's Ambassador Program. Annetta is a certified mastery coach and a certified trainer. She is an award-winning journalist with more than thirty years' experience in the broadcast industry. Visit her website for your free report on three communication mistakes that may be costing you business and relationships: **www.SpeakWithEase.com.**

About Cynthia Mabry

Cynthia Mabry is radiating with joy as she has truly found her transformation platform in her home-based business. Formerly in telecommunications, Cynthia reinvented herself after her personal and professional lives halted in 2008, following the untimely passing of her husband and shortly after being downsized out of her career. Today she is an inspirational speaker, marketing strategist, and choice advocate. Her candor about her life's events coupled with her tenacity and successful reinvention of her life has truly struck a chord and is creating a movement across the country. Cynthia is committed to being the source of inspiration for others to make a change and regain control of their lives through choice and financial freedom. Visit her website: www.StraightHappy.com.

www.ingramcontent.com/pod-product-compliance
Lightning Source LLC
Chambersburg PA
CBHW060141050426
42448CB00010B/2242